CW00368909

BLUE SKIES
IN TUSCANY

Selected Poems

Hugh David Loxdale

BRAMBLEBY BOOKS

BLUE SKIES IN TUSCANY: *Selected Poems*
Copyright© Hugh David Loxdale 2003

All Rights Reserved

ISBN 0-9543347-2-8

First Published by Minerva Press in 2000

Published 2003 by
BRAMBLEBY BOOKS,
Harpenden, Hertfordshire,
AL5 5HE, UK.
www.bramblebybooks.co.uk

Cover photograph by Stefano Caporali
Author's photograph by Sinead Lynch

Printed in Germany for Brambleby Books by
*AZ Druck und Datentechnik GmbH, Postfach 3150, 87440, Kempten,
Germany.*

BLUE SKIES
IN TUSCANY

Selected Poems

By the same author:

The Eternal Quest (1988), Merlin Books Ltd.
(under the pseudonym Hugh Llewellyn);
Re-published 2003 by Brambleby Books
(under the name of Hugh David Loxdale)

Fascinating Felines (2002), Brambleby Books

Bird Words (2003), Brambleby Books

This book is dedicated to Nischi

About the Author

Hugh Loxdale was born in Horley, Surrey and is of English, Welsh and Irish descent. He was educated at Apsley Grammar School, Hemel Hempstead, Hertfordshire and Reading and Oxford Universities and has been interested in natural history since a very young age. He is an entomologist by profession. Presently, he lives with his wife in Harpenden, Hertfordshire. This is his second collection of poetry. The first collection, *The Eternal Quest*, was published under the pseudonym of Hugh Llewellyn by Merlin Books in 1988, and later re-published under his own name by Brambleby Books in 2003.

Preface

The majority of these poems were written in England over the past fifteen years, although one goes back much earlier, i.e. *Railway Elegy* (15), written at Hemel Hempstead, Hertfordshire in January, 1970 and revised 1984. Some had their origin during trips abroad in the 1990s, e.g. the eponymous poem after which the selection is named - *Blue Skies in Tuscany* (57).

Poems 1-2, 5-7, 11-14, 16-25, and 44 were written whilst I lived in Hemel Hempstead during the years 1985 and 1986; poems 4, 8-10 were written in 1987; poems 3, 26-38 in 1988; poems 39-41 and 49 in 1989; and poem 42 in 1990 whilst I lived in Flitwick, Bedfordshire. Poems 43, 45, 50-54, 70-71, 74-76, 79, 81-84 were all written in Harpenden, Hertfordshire during the years 1994-99; poems 46-48 at Hartland Point, north Devon in 1996; poems 56 and 60 in Tucson, Arizona, USA in 1997; poems 57-59 at Rignana, near Greve in Chianti, Tuscany, Italy, also in 1997; poems 55, 61-69 in Bavaria, southern Germany in 1998, and poems 72-73, 78 and 80 during a recent holiday to the islands of St. Kitts-Nevis, West Indies (where some of my maternal ancestors lived from the late 17th to early 20th centuries), in the autumn of 1999. The poem *Blackcap* (77) was written during a short visit to Antibes, southern France in April, 1999. The *Railway Elegy* (15) refers to the railway line and station at Hemel Hempstead, the so-called 'Nicky Line', during the mid-1960s, *The Castle* (35) to Beaumaris Castle on the island of Anglesey, Wales, which I visited in September, 1988 and previously.

The poem *Thrips* (1, revised 1993) was dedicated to Professor Trevor Lewis on his retirement in 1993 and is reproduced here from *Thrips as Crop Pests*, edited by Trevor Lewis, with kind permission from the dedicatee and CAB International, Wallingford, Oxon., UK.

Hugh D Loxdale, 22 January 2000

Preface to this Edition

Blue Skies in Tuscany has been published in this second edition by Brambleby Books, which specialises in natural history, poetry and leisure.

Contents

Thrips

Thrips...
Tiny, shiny
Black snips
Of life
Whose main claim
To fame
In the world
Rests
Because they are
Injurious pests
Infesting cereal
Crops,
Onions, peas, fruit
And ornamental flowers.
The thunderflies
That fill
Sultry summer skies
With innumerable hordes,
Occasionally
Causing strife
By alarming plant
Growers,
Irritating skin
And getting in
Ears, nose and eyes...
Whilst most
Contrary of all,
Squeezing themselves
Behind picture, frame
And glass,
There to die...
A bizarre

17

Habit
Which can annoy
Nearly
Beyond words.

Halley's Comet (December, 1985)

I can hear rain falling
Outside through
The dark December night...
Which means that the sky
Must be cloudy,
Enough to hide Halley's Comet,
Apparently,
According to official data,
Now at its best
Viewed from
The Northern Hemisphere,
Although, in fact,
A wonder of nature
Much to deride,
It being so feeble
Against the celestial rest
As still to be invisible
With the naked eye.
Truly, unless it improves
When next it should appear,
I fear it's not worth the candle
Waiting another lifetime
To see
This gadding lump of matter...
A comment sounding niggardly, yes,
But one which,
From the comet's present showing,
Is disappointingly right...
Unless, of course,
It glows bigger - and brighter
Yet!

The Cat

A most excellent invention is a Cat,
With its handsome features, sleek coat
And hazel eyes,
And very good company too; most happy
For a chat…
With the added advantage (some would say)
Of being a good listener,
Giving few replies!

The Belles of Westoning

Every working day,
The belles of Westoning
Stand on the corner,
By the shop,
Waiting for the bus.

Only two of them,
They wait, mostly silent,
Without complaint or fuss
In the bitter winter air.

Both exceptionally beautiful,
Perhaps they are good friends.
True to say, whoever wins
The hand or heart of one or other
Will be a lucky man indeed;

Unless he has a friend too…
And between them,
They win the pair!

When Charm Turns Sour

When charm turns sour,
It is as a lovely flower
Replanted in poisoned soil,
Whose bright petals at first discolour,
And shortly thereafter, despoil.

Impassioned Love

Impassioned love
Is unreasonable,
A kind of insanity,
And can be just as hurtful and unfair
As intense hate,
The reverse side of emotion…
Both unstable states
Produced when souls,
Like roving worlds,
Either caress
Or collide.

Possession

What on earth
Is the worth
Of great possession?
The obsession
With accruing
Material wealth
At the expense
Of health
And life,
When the whole
Wide, colourful world
Waits unexplored.
It is to be deplored
Especially,
That millions groan
About the millstone
Around their necks,
And age
Whilst the mortgage
Still is paid...
Only to find,
More's the pity,
That when this is achieved
They have been deceived...
That bricks and mortar,
However strongly laid,
Are transient...
Like the wind,
Whereas the expansion
Of one's Soul
Is a goal never bettered...
This glorious thing,

Heaven sent,
Which, with the wind,
Has no shape
And cannot be seen or rent,
Yet may eventually escape...
To live on, unfettered,
Throughout eternity.

Let's Not All Get Killed

Let's not all get killed,
The amateur along with the skilled,
As we hurtle into stagnant mist,
Love-ones forgotten - Oh caution desist!

What is the point of this urgent rush?
Why death's face do we happily brush?
Why this joy to overtake -
Even cars of the self same make?

Does it matter that we arrive so soon
With engine whining - a harsh, forced tune,
Having risked life and limb - best possessions,
Just to indulge such brief obsessions?

Much better to respect mist, car, lorry,
Better now......safe than sorry,
And perhaps live out good years, long-filled
Than end today with warm blood spilled.

Was My Love For You

Was my love for you
As this scene -
Mysterious and serene?
Or was it merely false and shallow
As the fields beyond - cold and fallow?

This you may never know
Since such clear thoughts are lost
And uncertain...
Like those wandering birds
Which once flew straight and true
Across familiar tracts,
But now reach instead,
Unwittingly,
Rich, distant lands anew.

Rings Beyond His Feet

On a telegraph wire a Blackbird sings,
Oblivious of the many rings
That pass below his feet.
Only his own melodious calls
Does he hear...
A glad, joyous tune which befalls
The distracted listener...waiting for friends...
Or other things...

Written in the garden of the Fox Inn, Harpenden,
on a dull, rainy evening in early June, 1987.

Homeward Bound

A full, luminous Moon rises in the east,
A weak orange Sun sets in the west.
The air temperature is extremely cold,
The daylight noticeably fading,
The land quiet and deserted.
No noise of owl,
Fox, deer, hound,
Or any other bird or beast
To test one's skill,
And nerves.
Only the hushed
Sound of my footsteps,
My breathing
As I head homeward
Up Farm Lane,
The last steep stretch
Completing a rushed
Winter stroll.

A Perfect English Rose

A perfect English rose,
Amber coloured,
Joy to the eyes and nose,
Stands on the window sill
In a jam jar
Half filled with water.
My friends laugh and say
'Fancy putting a gorgeous bloom
In a vessel so prosaic'.
But the flower's beauty is such
As to transcend
The ordinariness of the vase.
Likewise with the young woman
I met recently
Whose bright radiance
Outshines the inadequacy
Of any poetry or prose.
She unquestionably,
To my mind also,
A perfect English rose.

Security

This firm
Security we seek
In home and job,
Is it not a false god
Worshipped by ages
Of pilgrims who have trod
Weary miles
To find it?
Surely, the greatest
Mountains
Erode away
Bit by bit,
Whilst lesser piles,
The ancient palaces
Which have bust
The coffers of Emperor-
Kings,
Soon return to dust.
Nor is the written
Word safe
From the ravages
Of time,
Paper particularly,
One of those things eaten
In good faith
By innocent worm
And moth alike.
Only love and DNA
Endures,
The first, a true happiness,
Lasts a little while,
The second, derived

31

Therefrom,
Passed down
Family lineages,
Persists considerably
Longer;
Although even this
Is not fixed,
The genes being reshuffled
And random mixed,
As in each nation,
Generation succeeds generation,
Allowing adaptation
To changes which, silently,
Select the stronger
From the weak.

Small Boy on the Rocks

A small figure huddled on weathered rocks,
Sitting contentedly minus shoes and socks,
Gazing far out over a placid sea,
Lost in thoughts of calm certainty.

In some ways, I wish I could be he again.
Not that I want to turn back the clock's
Restless hands,
To re-explore such misty,
Half-forgotten seas and lands,
But more especially - to re-attain that state,
Now dimmed,
Bordering on equanimity.

Railway Elegy

The rusty track trembled...
Then ran toward perspective
And the town...
Leaving in its wake
Much silence,
A few oak sleepers scattered by,
And assorted pebbles,
Worked smooth, long before,
On some abrasive Sussex beach.

All around, young ash and elm
Swayed vigorously in a gusting breeze
As though the ghosts of trains rushed past...
Thin, supple limbs raised skyward,
Defiant, mocking the rails
Upon which Man's leviathans once moved.

Further down line,
Dappled with flickering green
Of shades cast by gentle light,
Mossed, hidden in new sprung trees,
The crumbling station lay,
Stripped of its roof,
That damp, encroaching ferns
Grew amidst the rubbish on the floor.

Here a melancholy dwelt,
More desperate to survive
Than the bindweed struggling up
To catch faint spirals of the Sun.
Despair sustained by lingering death
Where, but ten years prior,

Hissing locomotives had steamed
Along this line
That now to wild returned.

And thronging the platform
Deep fissured,
With thistle and yellow ragwort
Thickly sown,
Mixed, milling post-war crowds,
Exhilarant in the summer heat,
Had awaited that brief time
When sweet anticipation
And grimy, puffing reality coalesced.

Smart businessmen,
Relatives departing,
School children,
Mothers with sticky infants
Off to the seaside or zoo;
Whilst the smoke-filled air
Charged both with soot - and hope,
Swirled about acceptably...

Although soon to disperse,
As the chapter's close
And progress's quickening pace
Steadily blew away
The inspiration of a former age,
Replacing it
By clean, efficient, unloved uniformity...

If not,
Then bequeathing it,
As at this spot,
The sad inheritance of weather...
And thriving wilderness.

What We Are And Might Become

What we are and might become
Is generally of little consequence
To those who follow us
Remembering, at most,
A name
And perhaps a deed,
When they strive on anew,
So fresh and keen,
Seeking experience, wealth or fame,
Until they realise
Their time is draining too…
Whereupon, of the past
They take more heed,
Hence emphasising the need
Not to indulge greatly
The future,
Only the inconstant present sense;
The sum worth of ever fleeting reality.

Love's Last Embers

The love that for you alone I bore
And which once raged within me
Like a forest fire
Threatening to engulf all before,
Has now gone out,
Smothered by your seeming cold desire.

However, as the love-light ceases,
A faint glow is still seen
Amongst the dark ashes,
Brightening as the wind of change
Increases,
Showing that affection, at least, has survived
The ruin of this most unlikely dream.

The Meeting

One more quick
Saunter around Green Park,
Then I must be away…
To the Meeting.
No time to infuse
The view
Towards Piccadilly,
Watch reassuring pigeons,
Or for eating.
No, because I am duty bound
To attend at two,
Now fairly soon,
And embark
Into a grand building
Up the staircase
To face
The next leg
Of my journey,
One influenced
By a new set
Of strangers…
I have never met,
So that it is
Impossible
To know
Where it may lead,
Much less,
How it will end.

It Is Not the Same

On Thursday, a fine day,
Young swallows on thin wires assemble.
None shows fear nor tremble
At the awesome journey ahead.
Only instead
They preen, twitter
And make short flights,
Achieving new heights
In aerial display.

By Sunday, the wires are bare;
Little is left to reveal
Once their presence there.

The Sun shines; the hour
Is pleasant enough,
Although I can't enjoy it.

It is not the same.
A spectator, I watch the arena
Sadly empty, now that
The players are gone
Along with the game.

What Wonderful Things Are Trees

What wonderful things are trees!
Taken largely for granted
Because one sees
Them so commonly.

I realised this
Whilst on the train
Going to London
In squally rain,
Looking through the window
At the passing scene
And observing
Their variety
And lean,
Naked beauty
Planted amongst
Square, plain
Buildings.

One in particular
Caught my attention,
An immense Oak,
Masterpiece of design
And engineering,
With spreading
Branches heading
Out generously
All around.

My instantaneous thought was
'How strange a sight
Such objects are', -

Huge, towering filigree
Skeletons
Dotted over the landscape,
The quiescent framework
Of organisms
That in spring and summer
Produce a fluttering mass
Of temporary green structures -
Leaves -
To sequester light,
Shedding these
Only as dark and cold
Return.

Each year
The skeletons grow bigger...
Then age wearies them,
Elements and decay
Weakening the fibrous grain,
So that they finally,
One day,
Crash to earth...

Near their descendants,
The newest of which
Also presently rest
On the ground
As small, unopened packets,
Encapsulated vigour,
Lately spilled
When autumn
Wavered in the face
Of a keen
North wind.

A Face So Fresh And Young

This raw autumn morning,
Whilst out walking
Past evergreen
Pines
Near the park,
I saw a face
So fresh and young,
The loveliest
I have ever seen.
A girl, perhaps sixteen
Or seventeen,
Not older,
One no man has sullied,
Nor the years condemned.
A fair beauty, who, later on,
With colder looks
Than she cast me,
Will break many a heart,
But whose rare features,
For the moment,
Are largely unknown and unsung,
Either in books,
Music or any other art,
Save for these
Scant lines.

November

For the brave majority
Who decide to remain
And see the winter through,
November cannot be insured against,
It must simply be endured.
Thirty days
When rain, sleet and snow,
Often carried on
Unbridled winds,
Rule supreme.
Short, dull, dire days
Which seem
Endless in their spite,
Made tolerable
By the roaring
Evening fire indoors
And the thought that
Relatively soon -
After Christmas -
The Sun, long in decline,
Will slowly regain its strength,
At length again
Filling the world
With flowers, soaring insects
And singing birds,
Lured back to the vacated stage
By those twin life givers,
Warmth and light.

Man and Woman

If the chemistry
Between man and woman
Is not there,
Then shed not
A superfluous tear;
Only accept
The unpalatable fact
Before ever
Signing a wedding pact,
And take good cheer;
At least
You are still free!

The Big Surprise!

Into that familiar face
Where once
Not a blemish ruled,
A few coarse lines appear,
And some grey hair,
Which were decidedly not there
When last they looked:
'Can it be true?
Am I mortal too?'
They ask
Whilst continuing to stare
At an alarmed reflection,
Touching a crow's foot ...or a mole,
And lifting disturbed fingers
Through fading strands.

Why worry, it is only
The sands
Of time...shifting
And anyway,
On the whole
There's nothing much you can do
To change things.

So don't be fooled;
Enjoy Life's pleasantries
To the full,
Here, now...today!

Below Chepstow Castle's Towering Walls

Below Chepstow Castle's
Towering walls,
I pace the grass
In the Sun,
Pondering whether I shall
Indeed become
One of the many fools
Who, throughout history,
Have also done rash things
Hereabouts.

In my case, by
Rekindling
The amorous flame
Which once burnt bright
Within
For a beautiful woman,
Living locally,
Just across
The span
Of the Severn Estuary.

A bachelor girl
Who loved me not,
Neither would tell me go;
Thus leaving,
When our 'romance'
Ultimately waned,
Mystery,
And myself intrigued
To know

What deep-down she thought
And what, for my part,
I ought say or do
To win
Her fickle heart.

True, nothing ventured,
Nothing gained.
Nevertheless, for too long
She feigned
Affection, -
Love, kisses, tenderness - a lie?
Hence my
Reluctance
Now to rush back,
Which would be wrong.

On the other hand,
Can I actually pass
This way
And not try, once again,
To assail
That fortress strong - her mind,
Wherein kindness,
And real love,
May, I believe,
Yet be found?

Such notions as these,
Unsettled emotions,
Continue on circulating,
Around and around.

Homage to the Grave of Gilbert White

Down the meandering high street,
Past 'The Selborne Arms'
To the churchyard
There to pay
My salaams
And respects...to Gilbert White,
Long laid to rest:
Past the ancient Yew tree
Still growing strong;
Past hard grey walls;
Then sharp left
At last to find his humble grave,
Mossed and grassy sown,
Bereft of any adornment
Save for a small stone
At feet
And one at head,
The second bearing
The faint inscription
(To benefit the living, not the dead):

'G.W. 1793'....

And a few small flowers,
Tended lovingly
By a kind woman
Who discerns not
The flying morning hours,
Seeing me with a start
Against the glaring Winter Sun...

Whereafter
Having exchanged pleasantries,
She enters via a door
The quiet interior
Of the church,
Perhaps to arrange more bright
Flowers near altar, font and nave...
Although I only
Assume this to be so,
For I do not follow,
Either to look inside
Or pray,
But immediately depart,
My homage done
This day.

The Task

Like ants,
We go about our allotted task.
Rarely do we ask
For what purpose
We toil so long
And hard.
Is it for 'Thy Will'...or our vanity
That we spoil what
Might otherwise be
A blissful life...
And bask
In the pleasant glow
That we do not know,
Only remain impelled
To do?

Is it through
Some dread urge,
The surge that swells
And pumps in our very veins...
A force
That cannot be held
Until we are spent?

Or do we, in fact,
Have free sway,
To choose any course,
However strange, any day?

I suspect not:
I fear we too
Are but poor creatures
That see the racing tide
And are swept along…

Except, that is,
For the odd Philosopher
Who, perforce,
By desire or luck,
Fate decants.

The Wasp

Ah yes, the Wasp...
That fearsome creature
Whose venom
True, is not
Often as deadly
As the Asp,
Yet even so,
Is a hurtful thing.

A smart insect,
Seen from spring
Through to the last call
Of autumn...
Though most commonly
When the apples
From the tree depart,
To fall
In September's golden age.

A lone wolf
That preys
Upon greenfly
And others...unsuspecting...
Scouring the herbage
For a tasty meal
To feed its sisters
Back home, still
In their childish stage...

And occasionally,
To have a sip of beer,
Or jam,
With us here
At the table...
Which I enjoy...
Though with a few,
Precipitates, quite dramatically,
But a fearsome fuss...
Or even rage.

The Cold

I have just gained
The most magnificent cold...
As impressive in its effects
As a heavy squall
That breaks suddenly
From behind the nearest
Fold of hills
To drench one
To the very skin,
First harbinger
Of some dread storm
To come.

And like a storm too
With its ominous claps
Of thunder - awful sneezes.
Rising to a crescendo
When one's patience snaps
With the torments
Of horrible affliction;
Eyes sting with coarse friction;
And nose streams forth
In incessant
Torrents...
Full wrath
Of a cruel assailant...
Much too small to see...
And yet, with a vile
And impudent hold,
A seeming endless misery
Before it finally eases,
Disappearing as quickly

As it came,
Back to Hades
Or on, ever on,
To afflict someone else
With the bold, unhappy same, -
A batch
Of noxious ills.

Greater Knapweed

Beside the sandy track
That leads from Steppingley
To Flitwick Wood
Greater Knapweed grows,
Though sparingly
It should be said.

Yesterday was such a flower,
Purple and fully open
To the midday hour,
And covered with butterflies,
Light and dark,
Probing and flitting
From head to head.

What should be done
To capture such a scene
In time?
To place on film,
Which might prove flat,
Or the Collector's press and pins
Both dated sins…and unkind?

Or attempt in abstract
Or flowing rhyme,
To describe this circumstance
Held in the substance
Of the mind
From a single glance…

Assuming these words
Can dance...
As the butterflies do...
Yet leave no trace
Of their passing,
Save the setting of seed
And with us,
A deep and perennial need,
Likewise lasting?

Lesser Burdock

Yesterday, whilst walking
Before the Sun lost
Its precarious hold,
I made the re-acquaintance
Of Lesser Burdock,
A plant I have not seen
For at least two summers.

No, it did not grab me
With a bur,
As if my clothes were
The hair
Or fur of some passing creature:
It was too early for that.

Instead, it held me
By its looks;
The flower heads, purple-pink,
And not unlike a thistle,
But with each bract
Forming clinging
Hooks below...

And the fact
That it was not alone...
But entertained
A swarm of butterflies -
Whites and Browns -
That sat lazily,
Sipping the feast
So provided.

Or occasionally, flapping
Their wings
In the warm, humid air...
Effort of supreme
Nonchalance on their part.

Now a day later,
With cool overcast skies
Threatening to soak
Everything afresh,
I may bemoan
That this incredible
Sight is temporarily
Kept from view,
With the butterflies
Absent, or extremely few...

However, I may also
Hearken at the thought
That should the Sun
Return,
The party will restart.

Whilst the plant waits now,
Only much later to mock
Those who visit
The countryside,
Using them merely
As a beast of burden
To transport its seeds
Elsewhere -
A tasteless and derided art...

Though one which, of necessity,
The Burdock needs,
Its fruit being spiky
And quite inedible.

Sweet Chestnuts

By Valley Farm
Where, only last year,
Two great Sweet Chestnuts
Stood proudly
Near the barn,
Their dark green, glossy leaves
Hanging like limp hands
In pendulous arrays,
Now just one remains.

The other is nothing
But a gaunt skeleton,
Which still heaves
Its huge branches skywards
To sample both sunshine
And the warm rains,
Although the feeling is gone.

And the life that haunts
Its bare canopy
Is a passing thing,
That rarely stays for long:

Starlings which produce
Their exuberant song;
Black crows that happily croak and caw;
And a fine Swallow
From the barn
Which lands briefly to preen,
Then takes wing,
And cuts
The air…once more.

What the Fuchsia Holds

At the centre of its silken sheet
A Spider sits, most discreet,
Waiting patiently through the sunlit hours,
Its web between red Fuchsia flowers.

And all around much traffic flows,
Of the trap this little knows,
Greenfly, hoverfly, bees and more,
Their first mistake, a last for sure.

Wales

Wales - to where
I now return each year.

A yearning, a persistent desire
That never fails
To call me back.

Land of my grandmother and her kin.

Land too, of proud mountains,
Valleys, rivers, pervasive castles...
And bleak forests...

Wherein prowl the
Ghosts of wolves, bears
And Princes
Long since slain.

Only the cry of an owl
Soon to kill;
Red kites that
Make even that consummate skill
A graceful art,
And the rarely absent
Wind and rain
Rise above
The music of cold, crystal waters...

These drawn from icy, ancient peaks
To tumble across shales
And shattered slate
Or granite

Where flecks of the purest gold,
Beloved by those that behold
But do not care,
Glisten like stars
Lost in the enormity
Of untidy Space...

And yet, beyond these
Urgent happy thoughts
Of Wales,
And the open window,
Speaks all that is left...
The real stars,
A thousand billion of them,
Alight still as the myths and legends
Of that mystic, magic place.

The Castle

This broken bastion
Of unrealised dreams,
Ancient and discarded now,
Was old when last I visited
Ten years ago - and again,
A dozen years before.

It has barely changed
These many years
At least to me, at all.

I stride the walkways
And battlements,
Consolidate the view
(Both within and without),
Inspect empty rooms,
Read the guidebook through.

There are no sounds
Of anguished men,
No cries, moans or tears…
Unless the vibrant call
Of the curlew
Or jackdaw close by,
Is their eternal echo
Long delayed.

It is broad daylight,
Sunny and warm;
Hence I am not afraid
To be here
Amidst so many ghosts,

If they exist.

However, a more disturbing
Thought does stalk
My mind,
A realisation
As much to fright
The soul
As any fleeting wraith.

On descending
Dark spiral stairs
Leading to overt green lawns
And departure,
A fickle thought occurs:

Am I searching for
The ghosts of men
Long since past I never knew
Or, more strangely,
Myself as once I was
In years now forever gone?

A subconscious quest
For youth, happiness,
Some intangible thing
That is as lost to me
As the thoughts and voices
Of they who once
Piled up and defended
These careless stones,
Back half a millennium
And more?

Unknown Heroes

Above scorched autumnal fields,
A Kestrel swoops - on mouse or vole.

When it rises, unsuccessful,
It is not alone,
Being mocked by small birds,
Wagtails probably,
Kind unknown.

Two in particular,
Bravest of the brave,
Persist in the attack,
Following every nuance,
Dive and veer,
Like air aces of long ago,
Defiant against a superior foe.

Surprisingly, the hunter
Eventually yields
To their lack
Of fear
And moves away...
Leaving two indistinguishable specks...
Victors
Of the day.

The Known Bird
(Lament for a black songster)

The Blackbird,
In jettest black
Who, six months prior,
Thrilled the Spring skies
With its matchless voice,
Now lies stilled
In the mouth
Of a pretty Cat,
Not out of choice...
Mainly bad luck.

One cannot condemn
The skilled hunter;
It is her prerogative
And desire.
Although I do decry
The bird.
That vision
Who brought such joy
And became complacent
To danger
Which is a tragedy...
And our loss too,
That beautiful, guileless creature...
Never again
To be heard.

The Stone

The Stone makes no decisions.
It is neither happy nor sad,
Hungry, good or bad.
It is never vexed by love,
Only by fierce heat
From the Sun above
And its equally severe
Departure later on.
It is washed by rain,
Groomed by wind and grit.
Its single action
Is to sit, to remain
Passively intact.
To be, rather than not.
And altruistically,
To provide attachment
For lichens and moss...
Perhaps on a wall...
Before Time, endless Time
Wears it down.
A gradual erosion
And loss of mass,
Until it is but
A speck of grit too,
Blown by the intemperate air -
Here and there -
To lie undaunted
By Life's cares
On seashore, river bed
And desert,
Grinding down its fellows
When at last...

All are molecules
Once again.

Litter Bug

The Litter Bug,
Unlike the Snail,
Does not leave
A glistening trail.

Instead,
It spreads an
Inglorious load,
Of cans and paper
Along the road.

Of sweet wrappers
In countless hedges,
And cigarette butts
On plush lawn edges.

Unconscious
Of its thoughtless roam,
The city is its natural home,
Although to the country
It often goes,
Where its filth,
It liberally throws.

A creature perhaps
Of too much affluence,
It strains to release
All its effluence.
And on and on it
Unwelcome gives...

70

A mythical beast?

Alas…it lives!

Fly Past

Towards the eye of God
Where the Sun breaks through,
The Jaguars roar
Two by two.

And onward, homeward fast they fly,
Hugging the veil of the blackening sky,
Back toward their distant base
With majesty, power, timeless grace.

Above the crowded land they speed
Yet subsonic still they heed,
Arrows to guard the tranquil nation,
Spectacle, pageant, peroration.

Oh happy band of men are they
Who wing the Heavens day by day,
Who encompass fierce mortal danger
To dice with death, the immortal stranger.

And when the ruffled peace resumes
And blackbirds deign to sing,
Those little specks, two by two last seen
Are lost...to the dazzling ring.

Here Is This Time

Here is this time
Seven years on,
And I am thus older,
And many are gone.

The berries are ripening,
The apples spilled,
Leaves turning yellow,
The morning air chilled.

And on towards winter,
With dull days a plenty,
Just one more season -
Oh were I again twenty!

Save for the Passing of Time

Save for the passing of Time
There is no reason or rhyme
For these words -
These cold, age-old, futile words -
Save for the passing of Time.

To see my signature on a record's sleeve
Bought yesterday, or so it seemed.
Never played, or once perhaps,
And now only can I relive
The desire of that act,
Now redeemed,
Save for the passing of Time.

When, by a peculiar whim
A library is searched -
Oh what the hell! -
For something bright, or dim, or true,
From what one once liked and knew,
Save for the passing of Time.

There is no reason or rhyme
Worse than the incessant
Tick of the Clock,
Striking out the minutes…and hours,
Or the faded signature,
One's own, dated so soon
Long ago…

And constant
As the flowers
That adorn sweet meadows
Or would be...forever...
Save for the passing of Time.

Autumn Days

The leaves turn brown and quickly fall;
The spiders spin their dewy webs;
The robin sings his plaintive song;
Mists and mushrooms gently rule.

Future Growth

Long after the farmer has retired
Whose men this very day
Armed with saw and axe,
Although disarmed of tears,
Destroy the remaining hedges
On the estate
And fell the large Ash tree
That of late
Inspired so many people
Over the years,
New trees shall grow
To spread and flourish
On this land...
In an age when there
Are no more fears
Of mourning such acts
Since they, as yet unborn,
Shall better know
And wisdom, not greed,
Then prevail.

For the Birds
(To Christopher)

May you be able to
Tell a Turtle
From a Collared Dove,
Flying in the Heavens
Blue above.

A Song
From a Mistle Thrush,
That both sit on high
And sing
Gladly before the rush
Of urgent dawn.

And yet once,
A Coal
From the fawn Marsh Tit,
Hanging from a bough,
Whose words are oft scolding,
But beautiful...
And true.

Hartland Point

As clay in some
Giant's hand,
These rocks were
Buckled
Band on band...
That looming gateway
Between land and sea;
The grey cliffs
Before fair Lundy...

And when white horses
Dance and fume
Amidst turquoise waves
And towering spume,
Gulls soar static over
Breaking sheet;
Their wing tips to the
Waters meet...

And then off, up
Above the sheer,
Shadowed face
There to indulge
Another race...

Of windswept fields
At great cliff's edge,
With cowering bracken
And clipped sloe hedge...

Then at once the
Sun shone forth
From persistent clouds
For all its worth…

And far out in the
Shimmering bays,
Formed horizons
Of transient rays…
Like the radiant,
Focused gleams
Of the old Lighthouse's
Whirling beams…

And at this spot
We rest and stare,
Knowing at once
All Heaven's here.

Peregrine

Beyond the resolve
Of the human eye,
A Peregrine sits,
But will not fly...
On a cliff ledge,
Inaccessibly high,
Far from earth
And near the sky.

With sleek, slate wings
And white, grained breast,
It waits a further while
To complete its rest...
Until the Martins
Which gracefully swoop...
Are oblivious
To the loop,
The arc
That it transcends...
Now straight as a bullet.
That ends
With a strike!
And a lone feather,
Which descends
To the ground
Silent...
Without sound...
Above the rolling sea
And a distant, mewing
Cry.

The Beachcomber

I spied my love beachcombing
Down at the ocean's edge,
Her golden hair a glowing
As was her last made pledge...

To find some Ship's treasure,
Cast off on this rugged shore,
So that we may live in comfort
And work never more.

Alas, the beach was stony,
With little to reward the eye,
Save for the dramatic scenery
And the bowl of hazy sky.

As Time passed, with nothing found,
Her desire began to wane,
Until at length she plucked a pebble, -
'A Conglomerate' was her refrain.

And clutching this worthy triumph,
We struggled back for home,
My love for her eternal
Just as the tumbling foam.

The Lynx

Yes, indeed
To some
The behaviour of the Lynx
Is disagreeable
And stinks!

Cunning, predatory and cruel.

Yet then,
Is it not
The nature of the beast
To pursue, capture
And feast
On its hapless prey?

At least it is real,
Alive to the feel
And need of love and pain,
The Arctic wind and rain.

It is no mythical being
Standing on a marble plinth
To gaze down
Upon the world with disdain
And sterile aloofness.

I would say
It is true unto itself
In courage and in stealth,
And he (or she) who thinks otherwise,
Is but a fool.

Chestnuts of Apple Tree Field

In sixteen, some conkers fell
Into the autumn turf,
Far away from Flanders' Hell
And the blood-soaked earth.

It was in Apple Tree,
On land richly brown,
That saplings grew bold and long
And struggled from the ground.

Since that time, an age apart,
Whilst wars both raged and went,
And storms blasted the very heart, -
All anger, all passion vent.

And tall and strong these trees became,
Stretching to the stars,
Where song birds cried aloud their name,
Whilst below, lovers passed long hours.

And seasons and decades
Have swirled and cruelly swarmed;
Time and all its many shades
These monuments to life adorned.

Then as September beckons old,
A portent of the dark,
Their spreading limbs of brightest gold,
Enrich the morning walk.

Whilst silhouetted through stagnant mists
When Nature is quiet and stilled,
Their grandeur even so persists
In landscape bare and tilled.

Throughout the springtime - May and June,
After months of heavy grey,
These forms become a single bloom,
Huge pink flowers above the hay.

But now they are held as too mature,
Yet in their prime of strife,
Their future deemed most unsure,
Despite their zest for life.

If woodsmen saw with blades of rust
And crush with mighty blows,
And burn and render down to dust,
A dust where no tree grows.

What then shall we be left to see
In time that short is left?
Only fractured twigs - at least for me -
And memories…and birds bereft.

The Jogger

The Jogger jogs on through the rain,
Despite the anguish, or her pain,
Through the park with autumn tints,
Ever onward, she tireless sprints…
Every step, a milestone trod,
In her trainers, new fashion shod;
Her bright blue top quite wet and thin,
Clinging cold against her skin;
Along and down between tall trees,
She rushes past, as if she flees,
Pursued by all the demons known,
As the leaves about her blown
Settle onto the muddy path…
Past the Yaffles and their laugh;
On towards Hatching Green,
Where the Jackdaws caw and preen
Upon the plushest, sweeping lawn,
On she goes and then is gone…
Lost amidst the houses fine,
Where rich folk live and sometimes dine.
A fleeting beauty of muscular form,
Far above the aching norm…
Her name unknown, her route inferred,
Her pulsing breath…her only word.

Comet Hale-Bopp, March 1997

Hail Hale-Bopp, you shining drop
Of dust in the north, night skies!
Vagrant from the distant reaches,
Now radiant in our eyes.

Oh wondrous blob, with streaking plumes,
And many a tale to tell;
Herald of some awful doom?
Thus should we wish you well?

Or take delight in your passing by,
As you dip towards the Sun?
Our eyes transfixed, our passion met,
Your glory truly won.

We admire your sport, respect your grace,
Amidst the heavenly plain,
But fear your calling, if it's true,
As you wax and slowly wane.

So go back then towards that place
Where perhaps you had your birth,
And leave us to our sometime fate,
We here on little Earth.

Nischi

With hair luxuriant
And shot
With blazing gold,
As the radiant Sun
Awakening in the east;
Eyes, pure and blue,
The azure seen in
Soft, summer skies;
A smile as enchanting
As the flowers that first
Break amidst
The silent forest floor;
A voice, as mellifluous
As a bird apt to sing
Strange, haunting songs
From the loftiest bough…

And a kind, gentle soul,
And goodness too…
That rare, beauteous thing,
Which makes my love for you
As strong as words
Can say;
This is what I
Think of you
My dearest, darling wife
Above all else,
The joy and purpose
Of my life.

Hush, Let Us Not Weep

Hush, let us not weep
My darling Nischi.
My love for you
Is greater
Than the things
That make us sad.

Let us not forget
That spring will soon be here;
Do not the crocuses
Tell us so,
Whose odd,
Golden spikes
Now peep
Above the barren soil?

All we must do
Is love, rest and toil,
And then things
Should be well.

Glad days, and many
A happiness yet
To come -
All this is true
My darling Nischi,
Believe me.

As the dawn
Soon to awaken,
The young unborn
Whose many voices unspoken
Urge us…

Never to break faith,
Nor lose heart.
That like the
Speckled thrush,
Long unseen, but not
Forgotten…

A stranger may yet appear;
Loved;
A gift from God.

Andechs

'Come on, let's go to Andechs'
Was her refrain,
The large Monastery
On the far side of the lake,
High up, now shrouded in rain.
I was persuaded.
And so it was we went,
And boarded the ferry
To cross calm waters,
Still quite merry.

Yet it was truly not
A day to travel…
As the rains poured down
And pitted the water's surface,
As through a sieve.

It was rather a day
To remain
Curled up with one's warm wife
In bed, with a glass
Of rum at hand,
As she said.

Through steep streets we climbed;
Up through forests painted
By autumnal hues
Of red, gold and brown;
Past slippy logs
And toadstools rife;
Hollows and valleys
And much wildlife.

Eventually, looming above
Tall beech trees,
We saw the grey 'onion'
Dome of the Abbey tower;
That magnet with the power
To draw the crowds, -
But not via this
Tenuous forest route.

Our goal seemed close
And we climbed on in that belief.
Minutes stretched to tens
And many more.
Still the tower alluded us.

Though Jays screamed and danced
And caused the rain-soaked trees
To shed their load
Of droplets,
All seemed somehow quiet and remote
In a time and place
Where centuries had spoke,
But not left their mark.

By now, hot and tired,
We were transfixed,
Only to do
The one thing left
That we had
Strength enough to do:
Ascend the steps
That led to tranquillity
And the courtyard
Of the Abbey true.

Suddenly, we were there.
Through ancient doors
Into the dark baroque interior,
Not inferior
To the Wieskirche,
That masterpiece
Of gilded decadence;
To the hall
Of highly decorated candles
Some two metres tall,
Caged in;
And the tomb of Carl Orff,
Composer,
Eighteen ninety five
To Nineteen eighty two...
A plain tablet within the wall.

Lastly, to the restaurant,
With its strong beer
And excellent German fare.

Sometime past, or in the future,
We at last emerged
Into the freshest of air,
Whilst the rain came down
In torrents...

Back along the path
On, on we raced,
Soaked through to the very skin,
As was the land.
Back towards the town
And the old wooden quay...

Through black woods
And fading light
To catch the ferry,
Back across the Ammersee.

But it was too late.
'The bird had flown'...
So that we could only bemoan
Our plight,
And wait for the last boat
Of the season
At this hour -
Hoping that it would come
More certainly than the Sun
That never shone
All day.

Even so, a sense of fun
Pervaded,
And we laughed
At what we had achieved.

Hummingbirds

Here on Mount Lemmon's
Higher peaks,
Where now
The wind only occasionally
Speaks through fir and pines,
The contents of Nature's jewel box
Have been spilled...
Those little animate specks
That have thrilled
Many a passer by,
Including myself:
The hummingbirds,
Adorned in brilliant hues,
With glittering feathers
Of green, purple, black and red,
Their long beaks
Piercing the forest flowers...
And then, in an instant,
Gone - at the blink of an eye -
Back to the cloudless sky
And the dark wooded edge.
An illusion of the purest kind.
One that haunts the mind,
And inspires the question:
'Was what I saw true?'
Here on the lonely
Peaks of Mount Lemmon,
Halfway up towards Heaven,
Where these tiny angels dwell.

Blue Skies in Tuscany

Blue skies in Tuscany,
Distant curving hills,
Cypresses and olive groves
And flower-strewn rills.

Villas and oak trees,
Old and evergreen,
Swallowtails that dance the hours;
Small lizards rarely seen.

The Oriole's lone recital
From a shaded bough;
Soft, warm breezes
That waft the cloudlets slow.

Lilac and yellow broom,
A splash of brightest hue;
Large, dark metallic bees
That visit swift and true.

Hot Sun and strong scents;
The grasshopper that rasps its joy
Amidst the lilting grasses
That beckon and alloy.

A scene indeed so tranquil,
As if it were but dreams;
Here where the senses mingle
To prove all *is* what it seems.

The Wait

It is a very different day.
Yesterday was hot.
The air was full
Of butterflies and bees,
And the songs of many birds.
Today, it is still and overcast...
The hills are misty and restrained.
Only a goldfinch sings
Cheerfully from the
Tall pine tree,
From whence cones fall
Sporadically and hit
The ground.
The dog, a large brown hound,
A hunter by inclination,
Breaks up the cones in
Its soft mouth.
The children speak in several tongues.
The clouds,
Thicker than this morning's,
Still let through
Their warming rays
To burn the tender arms
Of Englishmen.
A deckchair remains
Empty
Now that the adults are few.
Only we are left
On this blanket,
A raft on a sea
Of grass, clover
And dry oak leaves.

The hours seem longer
Than ever.
I can smell mint…
Despite the blood orange
That we ate and enjoyed.
We all are waiting, but for what?
Perhaps it is for deliverance…
Or someone to take us
To Siena?
We are content.
Whatever, we will soon eat dinner.

A Meadow in Tuscany

Within the rhyming
Grasses, a meadow
That unfolds
To yield a stand
Of brilliant yellow broom
And the most classical
Of views imaginable...
The wild flowers
Compete in profusion.

The tall gladiolus,
Cerise,
And beyond comparison -
Orchids, trefoil, clover,
Anemone
And pink thyme...
A delight to behold,
Planted in sublime confusion.

But this is not all.
Here the butterflies play...
Browns, whites, yellows and blues.
As many as one could
Wish for to while away a day.

Later, the grass cutters arrive,
Tanned and keen.
Men of the land.
They do their job well,
Earning every lira
That is due.

I can hardly bear
To visit the scene....
Nor the barren stubble,
And the few butterflies that remain;
Survivors of an essential task -
Bringing in the hay.

And who is to say
Otherwise...
Except for the timing?

When shall we return to Tucson?

When shall we return to Tucson
With its mountains, alluring and dry;
Its vast, searing desert
Beneath the endless sky?
Its Cholla and Ocotillo
And Paloverde trees,
Which cast their graceful shadow
Through the hot, restless breeze.
And Cactus Wrens and Flickers
With loud and piercing calls
From Mesquite and Saguaros,
High up on valley walls.
Prickly pears and desert flowers,
Lizards and butterflies,
Rattlers in shady cracks,
Where all coolness lies.
And especially its good people,
Rugged and enduring too,
Who have built this bold oasis
Amidst the desert true;
Part-tamed this lonely landscape,
With its harshness and many thorns,
Who erected fine buildings
With verdant, springy lawns.
A testimony to courage,
A will to overcome,
Where motorcars appear the king
Under the tireless Sun.
Yet where water, in fact, holds the key
To life of this bursting town,
Where brown and green still wrestle
To wear the winning crown.

May we come back to
This place one day
To find it alive and well,
Where water now flows and tumbles
In each plaza...and glistening mall.

Don't Shoot the Coot

Please don't shoot
The Coot;
It's a nice bird really.
With its sleek black livery
And snowy cap,
Bobbing gently on the lake;
Occasionally submerging
To take a piece
Of stringy weed
To satisfy a hungry need.

Its voice is not very musical;
Not at all like a flute.

More of a car horn
As it sounds off,
Shrilly, about
Territory and mate.

Certainly compared
With the grey swans
Upturned nearby,
It is rarely, if ever,
So mute.

Orange Hibiscus

I sit on the veranda
On a rainy day,
Smoking a cigar,
Watching the platinum lake
One way,
And the birch trees,
Tall and fair,
At the edge of the garden
The other…
Hoping to see
An exotic bird or two…
But there are none
Since the rains began
This morning.
The wasps continue
To forage on the orange Hibiscus;
It is apparently too cold for bees.
Several times I hear strange calls
From the woods
Beyond the birch.
Probably woodpeckers,
Great or Lesser Spotted,
I do not know.
The clouds begin to lift.
The train glides by
In musical rhythm,
A distant echo.
Maybe the Sun
Will yet break through.
The Hibiscus are themselves
Small suns,
Clustered and glistening

In a field
Of dark green leaves...
They provide
The inspiration for these words...
And another rum...
To keep out the damp...
With the flowers alone,
This cool scene
Is far from wasted.

Family Portraits

Looking at these pictures -
Your ancestors
Of long ago -
I can see you in them
Somewhere.
A piece, a slice, an image
Refreshed, re-minted
Quite anew.

Is it the cheek bones, lips or stare,
The ears, nose or rufous hair?

Is it an admixture
Of all these traits
And many more
That that library, the genome,
Has in store?

Your sweet smile, your goodly heart,
Kindness, intelligence, soul
And tender care.

Maybe those forebears
With their distant lives
In you, my dear love,
Their essence still survives.

The Garden at Utting

In a silence so profound…
The apples dropping to the ground…
With a thud…
Surprise and break the calm…
Falling amidst their fellows,
They do no harm…
Where the autumn crocuses,
The palest mauve,
Push up and defy the bombs,
The grass is tall and uncut
In places.
Most surprisingly of all,
I look up to see
A huge red shape rise
Over the garden with its loaded trees.
Little figures cling to the sides
Of the basket,
They wave to us below,
But look disturbed in their happiness,
Silhouetted so close, and yet so
Inextricably high,
In the declining light of the evening sky.
The flames whoosh
And illuminate the envelope
With a tangerine glow.
The object floats swiftly by…
More apples hit the mud.
Boys can be heard speaking
German loudly.
Then the silence closes
In once more.
There is no sound.

Red and Green Apples

Red and green apples on the autumn floor,
Scattered all about and juicy to the core.

A treat for wasp and human alike.
A sumptuous feast,
They may now rot whole; a terrible waste.

For the children who would eat them
Are far, far away...
Grown up and much too busy to play.

Unless these apples can be got
To the press and cider from them made,
Only the damp soil are they likely to aid.

Yet like fallen soldiers in that rich dust,
Their sacrifice is not lost...
If they give their promise...and for new life,
Their lust.

Orange Moon

At the fall of night,
With but a single star
And the hazy,
Orange Moon,
Squashed on one side,
Much as the fruit itself
Might be
To yield a little light,
Somewhere between
Full darkness
And the strength of twilight,
We watch the tranquil lake...
And the Moon's message
Reflected within it.
The sail boats creak and groan
Slightly along the green jetty,
Whilst the ropes slap
The mast heads tall,
In the calmness of the
Calmest breeze.
In this brief while
Some truth is revealed,
Although its form
Is not clear.
Maybe it is that
We are getting older
And must make certain
Of this fleeting world.
Or that we are not
Old enough
For the Moon...
To reveal its secrets.

The White Flat

The big, old flat
Is painted anew
Covering up traces
Where families grew.
The laughter, cries, singing
And sighs,
Here in this empty room
All history lies…
Concealed under a white-wash coat,
A history lost and quite remote…
So that now, an aura,
One so vibrant and live,
Can no longer, alas, survive.
Prepared, stripped clear
For the future bold.
Away, peeled back, the layers.
Old tiles, old paper, old floors,
All gone…
Regardless of cost,
A victory won.

The Marten

Under the eaves where nobody goes,
The Marten lives, sleeps and grows.

After midnight when the Moon is great,
His scurrying feet make quite irate...

Those who would gladly lay down their head
But who must now instead...

Wander the bedroom cool and dark,
And bang the ceiling or utter a bark...

To scare off this denizen of the wee small hours,
Who few have seen, but often prowls...

The land where once tall forests grew,
Although right now such trees are few...

And not half as cosy as below roof felt,
Where he can rest his luxurious pelt...

For whilst he seems a mythical beast,
Shy to make an appearance,
His scent betrays his whereabouts
Due to its pungent essence.

Hummingbird Hawk Moth

With hovering flight, the Hummingbird Hawk
Probes deep the fuchsias, its only work.
The whirr of wings above warm rain,
A sip of nectar, its only gain.

From gaudy flowers, red and mauve,
It steals its prize, thence to weave...
A sudden dash for the next bright patch,
Before our eyes can even catch...

Another glimpse of this blurred image...
Of orange and grey and apparently large...
A bird, a bee, a moth, who knows?
Save those who mark it ere it goes.

Across This Land

Across this land,
Ever dear,
Pretty England,
The great scar proceeds;
The slug trail of cement
And ashen grey,
Relentless in its needs;
Across little rivulets,
Clear and quiet,
Thick, lush meadows
Where golden cows
Munch their fill,
Only to be made ill
With leaden hay;
Across dulcet woods
Where fragile trees
Stretch in adoration
To the sky
And protect
The bluebells
And wood anemones
Far below
That can never
Struggle up and grow,
But die
As mighty juggernauts
And endless hordes
Of cars
Pass this way;
Across dales, downs
And valleys rich,
Where not now a single

Stitch of herbage
Can close withstand
Long the wild wind and noise
Of traffic;
Sears the tender tendrils
And young green shoots
Of England;
Her ancient birthright;
Solid oak and stone,
Parish church, pub,
And where old, sacred
Yews once stood;
Where bronzed men
In smocks
Bit hard against clay pipes,
And recounted proud
Tales of battles long ago
And peace;
Where children skipped
And played around
May poles fair;
And women cried
In labour and in cheer,
As church bells
Sang loud their peals
Of happy union;
Of grief;
Or accursed war,
And its atonement…
Past gravestones,
Lichen clad,
High above,
Where skylarks
Now never dare
To fly,
As torrid lorries,
Thunder by;

The butterflies
And bumblebees
That could thrive,
That may have flourished
Were the fields alive
With orchids,
Buttercups and bugle
Bright;
Of calm mushrooms
That glisten
Amidst the cool light
Of many a moonlit
Autumn night;
Waft by the silken
Wings of moth and owl,
Above the badger's angry growl.
If this great gift
Did once prevail
And might still,
Let it be cherished
Or become a memory
Lost…as dulcimer threads
Carried on the winds of time…
That no one ever knew…
Existed.

Commuting Angel*

You seem tired...
And your blue eyes
Are almost shut
On the busy trail.
You doze
Whilst a heavy head rocks
Gently in the sway
Beyond the sound
Of the headlong rush,
Back and forth, -
The gush
Of the long, dark tunnel,
Or opposing train,
Heard through the drifting scene...
The gold-brown autumn fields,
Sparsely peppered with sheep,
Your sleep
Is hardly interrupted,
And your beautiful, round face,
That of an angel
Of some kind,
Remains unperturbed...
Even as the journey draws
To its end,
You do not disclose
Your mystery...
As you awake serene
In your sober city garb
At Saint Albans.
And even with your loss,
Your memory remains
Pleasantly with me.

You alone have inspired
These lines.
You have fired
A longing to record.
You, you!
You unknown lady
Of this mortal plain,
Now gone without a word.

*Young woman seen on the train from London to Harpenden
at around 7.00 pm on Wednesday, 15th September 1999

117

Black or White?

Is black superior to white,
Just as some might
Say, the day is to night?
Or is it the other way around,
As the air is to the ground -
Certainly for creatures of that
Turbulent plain,
Who wing and dance
In the Sun and the rain?

Undoubtedly, each has its mark to make
In the hustling world,
In art, history, culture, politics, science;
Living for living's sake.

No one is better or worse,
Just adapted in a different way,
Indeed different,
There's the curse
Of Mankind,
That makes him blind
To both the darkness
And the light!

In the end, surely,
Variety is the spice of life?

Bat Moths

Amidst the oppressive gloom
Of the Nevisian forest
With its great buttress roots
Enveloped in strangling vines,
Its mahogany and palms
Penetrating, high up,
The pools of brilliant sunlight,
Brief victors of the retreating rain,
The silence is near absolute.

Here now, no bird, frog or insect calls;
The dark green, shiny leaves drip
Water onto the damp matted floor
Below and there can be heard
A gentle patter,
But there is no other sound.

In this strange, entangled place,
The Bat Moths -
Black velvet and as big as saucers -
Flit eerily through the canopy,
Often alone, sometimes in pairs,
They weave and dive
With funereal solemnity
Amongst the wet foliage...
Settling briefly on a leaf...
Only to disappear into the undergrowth
As silently as they first appeared;
These ghosts of the underworld,
Uninvoked, and sadly, so quickly gone.

They May Believe

They may believe
That their songs
Are new
And seamless pure,
Happy, melodious, true.
A cure for all ills,
Imagined or real.
But they do not live
In an empty room,
A vacuum free,
Without influence,
Without the key.
They are instead
Unknowing fired
With endless tunes and rhythms,
Songs of the restless trees
And beating rain,
Songs of summer and winter
And the north wind's pain.
Other birds, crickets
And grasshoppers few
Amongst the hedgerows
And tall, wispy grass.
The brash voice
Of human kind
About their daily course,
All mixed with
Careless force
Now lost beyond
The water's fall,
As the cruel
Chill turns west,

Whilst the child,
With her clarinet,
From the upstairs
Window is heard.
All fresh stuff...
And variety,
These young composers,
Each one...a jewel.

The Huntress

A figment of the darkness,
This was her hunting ground…
The small garden
Where the hollyhocks grew straight and tall
And lost their innocence…and hue
To the blackness
Where hardly a sliver of light
Now broke through
Beneath the still, rolling clouds
And the fickle stars
That refused to show…
To the bats
Whose shriek
Only she could hear,
Loud and clear…
The frogs that frequented
The pond
And splashed about, occasionally…
And on the lawn,
There she sat, paws withdrawn,
Waiting, waiting
For the first slight
Crack of dawn,
The first faint call
Of dove or swift…
Glaring amber eyes,
Staring into the hidden pitch
Where a mouse might twitch,
A moth beat its chocolate wings
In the heavy air, sticky as treacle,
And warm…carrying
The scent of roses and lesser blooms.

There she sat, all knowing,
All seeing
In her little world,
Content as any being
Can be…
Where the blackness reigns.
Black cat invisible
To those foolish enough
Not to see
Her low, breathing form…
Or those washed embers glowing.

Bird Words?*

Georgie, Georgie, Georgie, Georgie, Georgie.
Hello, Hello, Hello!
I know you're there!

Where are you, where are you,
Where are you, where are you?
Are you all right?

Coward......coward...
Phew! Phew! Phew!

Look, look, look, look, look,
Look, look, look, look...
I am not frightened...of you.
You know that, you know that.

You're a lunatic, you're a lunatic, lunatic, lunatic.

We know, we know, we know, we know, we know...
Show yourself, show yourself, show yourself...
You creep, creep, creep, creep, creep, cree-up...

You're just, just, just, just, just...
A peewit...ha, ha, ha, ha, ha!
You're cheap, cheap.
Look, look, look, look, look, look, look...
You all right? You all right? You all right?
You all right? You all right?

Look at me..., me..., meeee...
I can see you, see you, I can see you.
We know, we know, we know, we know.

Lunatic, lunatic.
Ha, ha, ha, ha, ha!
Creep, cheap, cheap, cheap, cheap.
Flutey, fruity, fruity, fruity.
Where, where?....

Georgie, Georgie, Georgie, Georgie, Georgie.
Wake up, wake up, wake up...
Brrrrh! Cheer up, cheer up, cheer up, cheer up!
Creep, creep, creep, creep.
You can nev...er win...cha, cha, cha.

We know, we know, we know, we know.
Give up, give up.
Creep, creep.
You son of a...cha, cha, cha.

Sink, sink, sink, sink, sink, sink,
You, you, you, you...
Why don't you...give in!
Give up, give up, give up, give up, give up, give up,
Georgie! Georgie! Georgie!

Wake up, wake up, wake up,
Where are you, where are you?
Look at me....Zzzrrr!

You lunatic, you lunatic, lunatic, lunatic.
Go home, go home, go home, go home.

Shout, shout, shout, shout, shout, shout, shout, shout,
Look at me, me, meee...e!

Are you still there.....Georgie?

---

*The voice of a Song Thrush, singing high up in a Sycamore tree;
Recorded 9th May, 1999

Blackcap

Alone amidst tall
Bay-laurel trees,
The cock Blackcap sings long
Its exuberant, deliberate song,
Not to please
The human ear,
But to declare to rivals strong
That it sees all!

The View from Cades Bay

Today at Cades Bay
I sit and watch
Waiting for something to happen...
As I stare out
Across the tranquil blue sea
That stretches, uninterrupted,
To the limits of the horizon...
To a strict line -
A demarcation,
Where the Earth shows
Not the slightest curve,
Where the dark waters
And pale, ruffled sky
Exchange shadowy tendrils
That meet the calm...

Waiting for a fish to jump;
A whale to breach;
A pelican to dive;
A sailboat to move;
A porpoise to show its
Beautiful, benign fin...

But nothing stirs...
Except the fascinating
Panorama of the clouds,
Shifting and re-forming
In endless re-statement
Of the artist's brush...

And then, just when
Tired tranquillity
Had lulled my mind
To restfulness,
The long green lizard
In the fig tree
By the wall
Darted fast away,
Such that the leaves trembled,
And shook free the diamond load
Of glistening rain
Fresh from the shower
That passed over Saint Kitts
And almost passed us by…

Walked deliberately down
The ropes of the vacant hammock
There to rest a while
And view the same scene
With its cool, reptilian eye.
An awareness, perhaps,
That all was not as it seemed…
And that the hurricane,
Still some distance off,
Was on its way.

Written at Cades Bay, Nevis, West Indies
13th - 20th October, 1999, awaiting Hurricane José.

Mobile Phone

You can never be alone
With a mobile phone.
Whether on mountain top,
In a valley,
Or on the languid plains,
You can continue
To be quite pally
With your boss,
Or the one you love,
Or both,
Far and near...
And keep up a happy discourse
Without fear
That your countenance,
Or location,
Will give the game away...
To reveal your
True pleasure, displeasure
Or even leisure,
Among the fields
Of golden buttercups...
Or in the busy, bustling,
Polluted street...
Clutching the hand-held bone,
With volume up
And voice raised a semi-tone,
As the bees
Or buses
Rumble past,
Necessitating perhaps a shout
To get the message out,
Free of the electric mains.

Mosquito Wars

The old tropical Sun has sped
From the western sky…
To leave a fearsome blackness
Of cloud…and a huge void
Dominated by the crescent Moon,
And a plethora of cold, majestic stars.

The air vibrates to the rhythms
Of tree frogs and the cicada's song.
The small, once bright green lizards
Peruse the walls and dart
Vertically in search of insect fare.

Now too, the mosquitoes,
With whirring engines,
Make their play…like Kamikaze!
And I am their victim!

Despite my whirls of cigar smoke
And felling of a few,
Their numbers are relentless.
Even thirty killed
On chest, legs and arms,
A sight that alarms me
And drives me away indoors,
Is nothing to them;
Just a casualty list
To be endured.

For they perhaps sense
That I cannot stay alert forever.
Soon the veil of sleep

Will blind my eyes
And they the mosquitoes - or at least
Some of their kith and kin -
Hidden within the confines
Of this apparent fortress strong,
Shall have their prize at last:
Fresh, warm blood,
Well worth waiting for
Considering their greed
And my relative size.

In the morning
My peppered ankles and thighs
Show the folly
Of my Pyrrhic victory over them…
And their desire to win
Whatever the cost… in dead…
Although unless they escape the room,
Their cause is likewise lost…
To propagate their kind.

The Sloth

A strange creature indeed is the Sloth,
Especially in its movement and growth;
It spends much of its time hanging upside down,
Whilst its fur is greenish and infested by moth.

Spring's Motive

Spring is beckoning!
The buds are opening out!
The Cuckoo hails his two-time call,
The Bluebells show full flower.

Chestnuts stand in majestic rows,
Their old crowns set ablaze,
Meadow grass grows lush and tall,
Whilst piebald cows fat graze...

And chew the cud beneath a sky
More daring by the hour,
As St. Mark's flies dance and gad,
So soon they are to die.

Along the hedgerows, above the woods,
The thunder rolls and grumbles,
Across the humid, pregnant air,
Amidst the Cranesbill bumbles...

The dark bees with their precious loads
Of pollen and nectar too
Returning to their secret holes
Known only by the few...

Who struggle on despite the threat
That still is some way off,
A torrential shower, both warm and wet
To make the young girls laugh.

PC

I am stuck
In front of the machine...
Slave to circumstances...
Exploring a world
Ever so big,
Peopled by six billion
Living souls,
But where never a bird sang,
A river flowed,
The wind blew,
Children cried,
Or dogs barked,
Nor cowards avoided strife...
Where never church bells rang,
Couples pledged their vows,
And sometimes kept them...
Seasons passed,
Snows fell,
Leaves grew,
On the oak tree and the fig...
As the tiny speck
Is hurled
Ever deeper into space
Around the gilded orb...
With too much radiation to absorb
Through the thinning air...
So very keen
To trail this well trodden path,
Whose social ills are hardly
Yet known...
Save by the people, like me,
Red eyed and tired,

Who have grown
Staring into the little screen
That now is our life…
And will be
Forever more,
Until
We are old.

Who Knows What the Weather Will Do

Who knows what the weather will do.
It may start grim and grey,
But soon the winter Sun comes out
To offer a lovely day...
And the Crocuses respond in kind
Under the naked beech,
Opening their fluorescent yellow blooms
To the pallid February sky.
Then again the wind turns cool,
The westerly clouds roll silent by
In the passage of an hour
The Jackdaws wheel and play,
Whilst by midday,
The heavens are dark and brooding,
Delivering their promise of rain...
So that the flowers
Close once more,
The birds cease to call,
And the sunshine is locked away.